D0681359

BEANObooks
geddes & grosset

Where do bees come from?
Stingapore!

Where do you take injured wasps?
To the waspital.

Why did the pear go out with the plum?
Because he couldn't find a date.

What's a wasp's favourite ice cream?
A hornetto.

What's the difference between a hippo with measles and a dead bee?
One's a seedy beast and the other's a bee deceased.

Why did Smiffy stand in front of the mirror with his eyes closed?
To see what he looked like when he was sleeping.

What do you get if you cross a football team with an ice cream?
Aston Vanilla!

Smiffy couldn't tell the difference between toothpaste and putty.
All his windows fell out.

Why is a football pitch always wet?
Because of all the dribbling during matches.

If you were surrounded by Dracula, Frankenstein's monster, a werewolf and a ghost, where would you want to be?

At a fancy dress party!

WHAT DO YOU GET IF
YOU CROSS A DOG WITH
A PHONE?
A Golden Receiver!

WHY DON'T THEY HAVE
TELEPHONES IN CHINA?
You might wing the wong number!

WHAT AWARD DID THE
INVENTOR OF THE DOOR
KNOCKER WIN?
The No Bell Prize.

Smiffy went to the dentist to get wisdom teeth put in.

When Smiffy went hitch-hiking, he left early to avoid the traffic.

Smiffy was listening to the match last night and burnt his ear.

WHAT'S ROUND, WHITE AND GIGGLES?
A tickled onion.

WHAT DO YOU GET WHEN YOU CROSS A HYENA WITH A BEEF CUBE?
A laughing stock.

What do you get if you cross an
elephant and a goldfish?
Swimming trunks.

**WHAT DO YOU GET
FROM A HUNGRY
SHARK?**
*As far
away as possible.*

What do you call a crab
with a red suit and
a white beard?
Santa Claws.

What's the
fastest thing in
the water.
A motor pike!

Which artist sits on ice cubes?
Botty-Chilly.

WHAT'S A FROG'S FAVOURITE FLOWER?
A Croakus!

What goes 'CROAK! CROAK!' when it's misty at sea?
A frog-horn!

What's black, rude and floats on water?
Crude oil.

WHAT DO YOU GET IF YOU CROSS A CITRUS FRUIT WITH A BELL?

An orange that peels itself.

Doctor, doctor. I think I'm a pencil. *Draw up a chair and we'll talk about it.*

11

14

WHAT DO YOU GIVE A DEAF FISH?
A herring aid.

**WHAT DO YOU
CALL A FISH WITH NO EYES?**
A fsh!

**WHY ARE FISH SO
SMART?**
*They travel in
schools.*

**WHAT'S BLACK,
SHINY AND TRAVELS
ROUND THE WORLD?**
Binbag the sailor.

What do you call a baker with red hair?
A ginger bread man.

Doctor, doctor. I've just eaten five red snooker balls, four browns, three yellows, a pink, two blacks and a blue and I don't feel well.
No wonder, you're not eating your greens!

Doctor, doctor. I feel like a packet of biscuits.
You must be crackers!

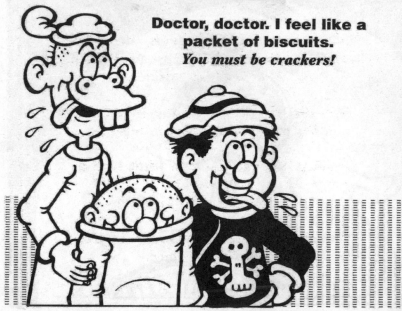

What do you call a cow eating grass in your front garden?
A lawn mooer!

What do you call a person who rolls in the mud then crosses the road twice?
A dirty double crosser.

Why did six planks stand in a circle?
They were having a board meeting.

Why is a red headed idiot like a biscuit?
He's a ginger nut!

What's an alien's favourite sweet?
Martian Mallows.

Doctor, doctor. I keep thinking I'm an aeroplane.
Come down to earth, man!

Doctor, doctor. Are you sure this cream will get rid of my spots?
Well, I can't make any rash promises.

Doctor, doctor. I've got a lake, a meadow and some trees growing on my cheek.
Don't worry. It's just a beauty spot.

Doctor, doctor. I keep thinking I'm a 40 watt light bulb.
You're not very bright, are you?

**What do you get if you cross a
parrot with a woodpecker?**
A bird that tells knock-knock jokes.

**What do you get if you cross a dog
with a stick insect?**
An animal that fetches itself.

**What do you get if you
cross a skunk with a
homing pigeon?**
A bad smell that won't go away.

Why was Doctor Frankenstein never lonely?

He was good at making friends.

What did the maths book say to the psychiatrist? *Doctor, I've got problems.*

I wish I'd been born a hundred years ago. *Why?* There wouldn't be so much history to learn.

SMIFFY WENT TO A FANCY DRESS PARTY AS A PIRATE...
... he wore a black patch over both eyes!

WHY DOES SMIFFY KEEP PET EARWIGS?
His ears are bald!

WHY DID SMIFFY CLIMB ON THE CAFE ROOF?
He heard the drinks were on the house!

SMIFFY GOT INJURED SWEEPING LEAVES.
He fell out of a tree!

23

What's always behind the time?
The back of a clock.

Why did they invent the wombat?
To hit the womball!

What goes DOT-DASH-DOT-DASH- NEIGH?
Horse code.

What opens doors and buzzes?
A bumble key.

What do you call an angry lion?
Don't call it anything. Just run away.

29

33

**Why are medieval
times called the
dark ages?**
*Because there were
so many knights.*

**What do you
call a very fast fungus?**
A mush Vroom!

**Why did the
skeleton go to
the restaurant?**
He wanted spare ribs.

**How did the baker get
an electric shock?**
*He stood on a bun
and the currant ran
up his leg!*

WHAT DOES A TEN FOOT TALL PARROT SAY?
Anything it likes!

WHAT HAPPENED WHEN TWO T.V. AERIALS GOT MARRIED?
They had a really great reception.

WHAT GOES HICK-HOCK?
A clock with hiccups!

WHAT'S WHITE ON THE OUTSIDE AND GREEN ON THE INSIDE?
A frog sandwich!

WHICH FAMOUS LADY RODE A CAMEL AND CARRIED A LAMP?
Florence of Arabia.

HOW DO DOLPHINS SETTLE ARGUMENTS?
They flipper coin for it.

HOW DID THE FIREFLY FEEL WHEN THE RAIN PUT ITS FIRE OUT?
De-lighted.

KNOCK! KNOCK!
Who's there?
DISHWASHER.
Dishwasher who?
DISH WASHER WAY I USHED TO SHPEAK BEFORE I GOT MY NEW FALSHE TEESH!

What does an envelope say when you lick it?
Nothing. It shuts up.

What do you call a man living in an envelope?
Bill.

Why did 'Erbert wear a cup over each eye?
Because he forgot his glasses.

Why did the boa constrictors get married?

They had a crush on each other.

Why did the dog have its puppies in a dustbin?
It said "PLACE YOUR LITTER HERE"!

WHAT DO YOU GET IF YOU
CROSS AN ELEPHANT WITH A SPARROW?
Broken telephone wires.

DID YOU HEAR ABOUT THE TWO DEER WHO
RAN AWAY TO GET MARRIED?
They antELOPED!

WHAT'S AS BIG AS AN ELEPHANT AND
WEIGHS NOTHING?
An elephant's shadow.

How can you tell when Smiffy's
in a car wash?
He's the one on the bike.

Why did Smiffy take a watering can
when he went diving?
To water the seabed!

Why did Smiffy
park his bike by his bed?
He was fed up sleepwalking!

How do you sink Smiffy's submarine?
Knock on the door!

44

What's red, sticky
and bites people?
A Jampire!

What do vampires
say when they're
being polite?
Fang you.

What kind
of letters
do vampires
get?
Fang mail!

How do you
flatten
a ghost?
*With a
spirit level!*

49

What do you get if you cross
Gnasher with a rose?
Something you wouldn't want to sniff!

What happened to the man who
made his dog walk in the gutter?
They both fell off the roof!

That dog bit my leg!
Did you put anything on it?
No, he liked it just the way it was!

What do you get
if you cross a dog
with a giraffe?
*An animal that
barks at low flying
aircraft.*

How do you
join Dracula's
fan club?
*Send in your
name, address and
blood group.*

Why do monsters find it
difficult to swallow vicars?
*Because you can't keep a
good man down.*

What do you call
a handsome,
kind and
charming
monster?
A failure!

TOOL
BOX

What's worse than an elephant on water skis?
A porcupine on a rubber life-raft.

How do hedgehogs play leapfrog?
Very, very carefully.

Why did the hedgehog say ouch?
He put his coat on inside out.

Why don't Dalmatian puppies play hide and seek?
They always get spotted.

Doctor, doctor. I think I'm a dog.
Lie on the couch.
I can't. I'm not allowed up on the furniture.

Doctor, doctor. My wife thinks she's a lift.
Send her in.
I can't. She doesn't stop at this floor.

Doctor, doctor. I keep seeing double.
Sit on this chair.
Which one?

WHAT DO CATS EAT FOR BREAKFAST?
Mice Krispies or mewsli.

**WHAT HAPPENED
TO THE MOUSE THAT FELL INTO THE
WASHING MACHINE?**
It came out squeaky clean.

**WHAT DO YOU
CALL A COW THAT LIVES
IN GREENLAND?**
An eskimoo!

**WHAT DO
YOU GET IF YOU
CROSS A SOLDIER
WITH A BIRD?**
A parrot-trooper.

HOW DO YOU START...

... *A cockerel race?*
Ready, steady, crow!

... *A cuddly toy race?*
Ready, teddy, go!

... *A jelly race?*
On your marks. Get set!

... *An insect race?*
One-two-flea-go!

... *A glow worm race?*
Ready, steady, glow!

What do you get if you cross a
shark with a dog?
An animal that barks at submarines!

What happens
if you eat
caterpillars?

*You get butterflies in your
stomach.*

Why did the pig
learn karate?
*So he could do pork
chops.*

What has fifty
legs but can't
walk?
Half a centipede.

59

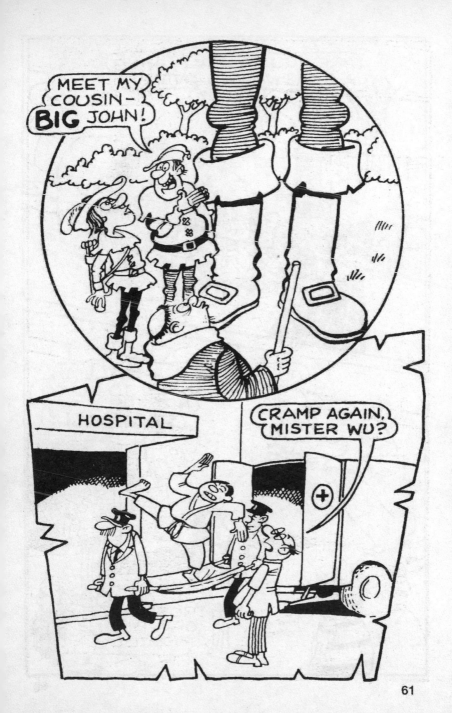

WHAT DO YOU CALL
A BOY WITH LEAVES ON HIS HEAD?
Russell.

WHAT SWEETS
DO FROGS LIKE?
Lollyhops!

WHAT DO YOU CALL A
LOST MONSTER?
A where wolf.

WHAT'S GREEN AND
SCALEY AND RED AT
THE BOTTOM?
*A dragon with
nappy rash!*

Where do you put a criminal sheep?
Behind baas.

What do you get if you cross a werewolf with peanut butter?
A monster that sticks to the roof of your mouth!

Which farm animals talk too much?
Blah-blah-blacksheep.

What's got a screen and wobbles?
Jellyvision.

What do you get if you cross a ghost with a boy scout?
Someone who frightens old ladies across the road.

What happened when the boy monster met the girl monster?
It was love at first fright!

What's a ghost's favourite game?
Hide and shriek.

Why do bees have sticky hair? 'Cos they use honeycombs.

What do you get from an educated oyster? Pearls of wisdom.

What do you call a lady balancing three pints of lager on her head? Beertrix

What do you call a lady balancing three pints of lager on her head while making a jug? Beertrix Potter.

Why were the elephants thrown out of the swimming pool?

They couldn't keep their trunks up.

What does an
alien say if
it lands in a
flowerbed?
*Take me to your
weeder!*

DID YOU HEAR THE
ONE ABOUT THE DUSTCART?
IT'S A LOAD OF RUBBISH!

WHAT DO YOU DO WHEN
THE M6 IS CLOSED?
GO UP THE M3 TWICE.

How do hens dance?
Chick to chick.

What happened to
the hen that fell
into the cement mixer.
It turned into a brick layer.

What do
you give a sick bird?
Tweetment!

What's yellow and
white and goes at one
hundred and fifty miles per hour?
*A train driver's egg
sandwich.*

DOCTOR, DOCTOR.
I THINK YOU'RE A
VAMPIRE!
Necks, please!

DOCTOR! I KEEP
HEARING
NUMBERS INSTEAD
OF WORDS.
*It must be
something you
eight!*

WHAT FRUIT DO
VAMPIRES LIKE BEST?
*Blood oranges and
necktarines.*

DOCTOR, DOCTOR. I THINK I'M A BRIDGE.
What's come over you, man?
THREE BUSES, FOUR CARS AND A LORRY.

WHAT GOES
ALONG THE
WASHING
LINE AT 100
MILES PER
HOUR?
*Honda
pants!*

WHAT DO GHOSTS LIKE TO SEE IN THE THEATRE?

Phantomimes!

What's a police dog's phone number?
CaNine, CaNine, CaNine

What historical events happened when the waiter tripped up at Christmas time?
The fall of Turkey, the overturning of Grease and the break up of China.

Did you know Smiffy was a triplet?
He's related to two short planks.

WHEN DO GHOSTS AND MONSTERS PLAY TRICKS ON EACH OTHER?

On April Ghouls' Day.

WHAT DO YOU GET IF YOU CROSS A JOGGER WITH A FOUR-LEAFED CLOVER?

A run of good luck!

What has eight legs and is see-through?
A black window spider.

Which reptile tells jokes?
The stand-up chameleon.

What do you get if you cross a centipede with a turkey?
Drumsticks for everyone.

How many insects does a landlord want?
Ten ants!

What do you do with fighting snails?
Let them slug it out.

What games do horses like playing best?
Stable tennis!

What do you call a chicken in a shell suit?
An egg.

Which famous painter always had a cold?
Van cough.

What do you call an inquisitive pig?
A nosey porker.

Doctor, doctor! I keep seeing into the future!
When did this first happen?
Next Thursday!

When is the cheapest time to phone a friend?
When they're out.

What happened to the man who stole a calendar?
He got twelve months.

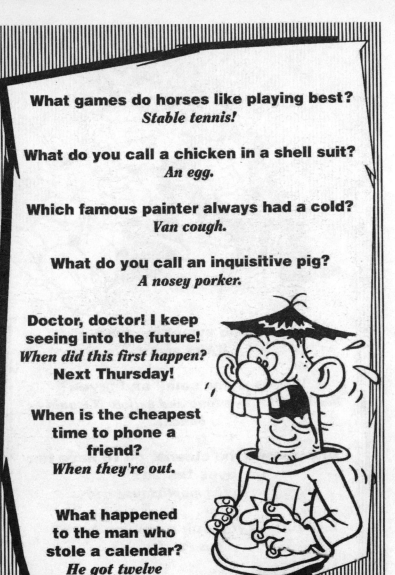

Which sweet moans?
Whine gums!

Why is a pea small and green?
Because if it was long and yellow it would be a banana.

Where does the cleaner go to have her eyes tested?
To the mopticians.

What do you call a singing herb?
Elvis Parsley.

Why do you call your fish "Explorer"?
Because he's been round the globe thousands of times.

What do you get if you cross a
giant gorilla with a cement mixer?
King Koncrete.

Did you hear about
the police football team?
They won the cop final.

Why was Cinderella rotten at football?
*Because she kept running
away from the ball.*

What do you call a rich rabbit?
A million hare.

What happens when a banana hits a strawberry?
You get fruit punch.

What do you call a two year old grape?
Mouldy.

What did the shy pebble say?
I wish I was a little boulder.

What grows in a field and makes music?
Popcorn.

WHAT WOULD YOU GET HANGING FROM A CHRISTMAS TREE?
Tired arms!

WHAT'S FASTER, HEAT OR COLD?
Heat, you can catch a cold.

WHERE DOES A DOG GO WHEN IT'S ILL?
To the dogtor's!

WHAT DOES A GHOST CALL HIS MUM AND DAD?
His transparents!

A SCIENTIST HAS CROSSED A DOG WITH A TORTOISE.
It goes to the shop every morning and brings back yesterday's paper.

What's 300 metres high and wobbles?
The Trifle Tower.

What exams do horses take?
Hay levels.

What has six legs and always does its homework?
A fly swot.

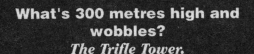

What cuts and waves?
A sea-saw!

Who lives in the desert and invents flavoured crisps?
Sultan vinegar!

HOW DO YOU GET FIVE DONKEYS ON A FIRE ENGINE?

Two in the front, two in the back and one on the roof going EE-AW-EE-AW!

What has a long neck and smells nice?
A giraffodil!

What's black and white and eats like a horse?
A zebra.

What does it mean when you find a set of horseshoes?
There's a horse going round in its socks.

WHAT DID THE FATHER BUFFALO SAY TO HIS YOUNGSTER WHEN HE WENT TO SCHOOL?
Bi, son!

IF YOU HAVE A REFEREE IN FOOTBALL, WHAT DO YOU HAVE IN BOWLS?
Goldfish!

HOW DO YOU KNOW OWLS ARE MORE CLEVER THAN FISH?
Have you ever had owl and chips?

WHAT DO BABY APES SLEEP IN?
APEricots!

WHAT DO YOU GIVE A PONY WITH A COLD?
Cough stirrup!

WHAT EXAMS DO GARDENERS TAKE?
Hoe levels!